Insights
for the
Journey

John Lucht

THE **VICEROY** PRESS

NEW YORK

INSIGHTS FOR THE JOURNEY: *Navigating to Thrive, Enjoy & Prosper in Senior Management*

Copyright © 2001 by The Viceroy Press Inc., The Olympic Tower, 641 Fifth Avenue 36D2, New York, NY 10022. All rights reserved. Printed in the United States of America.

Library of Congress Cataloging-in-Publication Data is available on request.

ISBN 0-942785-31-2   (hardcover) $19.95

"Your value is unlimited."

John Lucht

Also by John Lucht...

RITES OF PASSAGE AT $100,000 TO $1 MILLION+... *your insider's guide to executive job-changing and faster career progress.*

Unchallenged as America's and the world's #1 best-selling executive career guide for over a decade, RITES is now in a brand new and comprehensively revised edition. RITES has always been the definitive resource on working with executive recruiters. Today it also delivers the benefits—and minimizes the hazards—of using the Internet to advance an executive career.

RITES is accompanied by THE EXECUTIVE JOB-CHANGING WORKBOOK, which helps the seriously career-oriented executive implement the concepts in RITES OF PASSAGE.

Completing the suite of career tools from John Lucht is RITESITE.COM, a unique electronic resource which enables executives to display their achievements to the entire world (in identity-concealed resumes), make themselves known to the finest recruiters (in identity-revealed resumes) and find out about searches being conducted by the top-echelon firms who rarely publicize their searches except, in some instances, on their own proprietary sites.

"Your value is unlimited."

John Lucht

CONTENTS

Insights
for the
Journey

Insights
for the
Journey

A person ought to learn ***something*** in 40 years of business life.

Hopefully, I have. And hopefully, too, discoveries from my journey can help you on yours.

For 30 years I've been an executive recruiter interviewing and evaluating CEOs and chiefs of Marketing, Finance, Technology, Manufacturing, R&D and many other functions...initially with America's second largest search firm and, since then, with my own diversified search and consulting practice.

Earlier, I spent a decade as an executive on the fast track in corporate America. And during the past 12 years, along with recruiting, I've also done high-level outplacement and executive coaching.

But for now, let's think of me as your trail guide on a demanding trip through the wilderness...an observer who'll keep an eye open for your safety and offer some tips to help make the rigorous challenge you've undertaken more exciting, enjoyable and rewarding.

The metaphor fits.

You're engaged in a demanding situation I've seen others deal with in various ways day after day, year after year. Now let's share some of the strategies and techniques that have worked for the most successful of them. And let's avoid the predictable hazards that have tripped the unwary.

Here, boiled down to their essentials, are the best insights I'd offer if we were face-to-face.

Quite a few of these principles you'll agree with immediately, because they match what you're already observing every day.

Other points may seem surprising...perhaps almost outrageous...even subversive.

Give those ideas some serious thought. Regardless of how contrarian they may seem at first, when you reflect on them, they too will make sense. They too will square with your own experiences. Indeed, the points that seem most contrary to conventional thinking are potentially the most valuable.

Face it. We'd be wasting our time together if nothing here were different from the strategies and tactics everyone else already knows and uses.

So let's get busy. Let's share insights. On your part, even though I can't hear you, please do me this favor. Please silently talk back to me as we proceed. Challenge everything you read. Argue with me as we go along.

Do that, and the mental aerobics of the process will automatically add some calibrations to your own inner chart and compass for an exceptionally successful senior executive career. That's our objective, and you'll be surprised how efficiently we reach it.

Incidentally, there's a hidden bonus in all this. Soon you'll be using many of your best techniques of business leadership to improve other areas of your life as well.

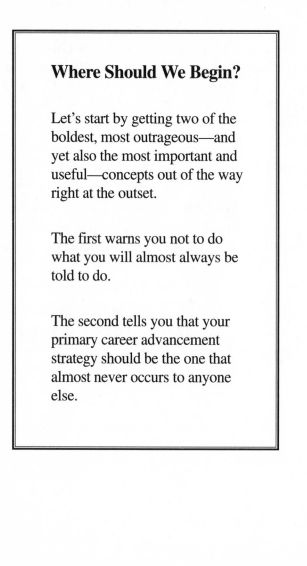

Where Should We Begin?

Let's start by getting two of the boldest, most outrageous—and yet also the most important and useful—concepts out of the way right at the outset.

The first warns you not to do what you will almost always be told to do.

The second tells you that your primary career advancement strategy should be the one that almost never occurs to anyone else.

Here's your #1 Mandate whenever you enter a new job in a new company...or take over the management of a new area in your current company:

FIT IN!

When you're hired or promoted into an existing organization—whether at the top or anywhere in the middle—your first and most important objective is to be accepted and well thought of by the people who already comprise the culture you're joining.

But, you say, you were told on the way in by the Board, by the CEO, or by your immediate superior that you've been hired to be a "change agent"...to wake 'em up and shake 'em up...to show 'em how it's done in a company or a department as successful as the one you've come from.

Still, you and your ideas need to be heard and

considered, not tuned out. And no matter how many people you may ultimately find inadequate and have to fire weeks, months or years from now, you cannot know who they are on day-one. Nor can you know who is capable of understanding, accepting, and *adopting* the changes you'll want to install.

Indeed, you won't even know what changes you *do* want to make until you really know what's going on. And you'll find that out a lot more easily if you're welcomed and defenses are allowed to crumble.

You are entering a *culture*. And no matter how dysfunctional it may be, if you come in with guns blazing, you will merely encourage the organization to sound an alarm. If that happens, the most useful people to your new regime—the ones who would have identified themselves and come over to your side as soon as they understood the merits of your thinking—will not be listening to it. Peer pressure will discourage them from siding with the stranger from outside, if you allow yourself to be perceived that way.

Exception: In the rarest of instances, you truly must avoid any rapport with the organization you join and totally rebuild it with outsiders like yourself. But *are* you in such a situation? Do you have the backing and the resources to pursue such an aggressive strategy? Is the organization utterly incompetent or corrupt? Are certain people unco-operative...perhaps even overtly disloyal? Does anyone have something to gain if you are not successful? Then, of course, you must "throw the varmints out."

But if the situation is any less dire, be cool, be approachable, be "one of us"...not an outsider... and be *successful*.

Your Nearly Inevitable Bum Steer

Almost always you'll get a mandate that—taken literally—sets you up for failure. The Board, the CEO, or another superior who has brought you in is very likely to exhort you to achieve immediate, noticeable change. "Let the chips fall where they may. Any change will be for the better." Often you'll hear powerful, unequivocal words.

Watch out!

The sad fact is that your refreshingly candid backer is likely to cut and run, just as soon as you get into trouble by taking precisely the strong approach that he or she suggested.

Example: An executive I coach was hired as COO

by a CEO who gave him a strong exhortation and carte blanche to "shake this place up from top to bottom. We need change, and plenty of it, and we need it now. I will support you in whatever you decide to do."

As we mapped strategy together, the new COO (who was preceded by several other COOs deemed unsuccessful under the same mandate) told me he intended to "hit the ground running" and "really shake up the place." The CEO would get the upheaval he asked for.

"Do that," I said, "and you'll soon be history, just like all the others before you." Instead, I urged the new COO, to make *fitting in* his first priority. "Go easy. Go slow. Observe. Be warmly welcomed before you take any action," I told him.

He took my advice.

Eight weeks after the new COO arrived, the CEO took him out to dinner and told him that his was the most promising entry anyone had ever made from the outside into this company.

And a year later, after the COO had delivered just two widely applauded firings, plus numerous well-deserved internal promotions, the CEO who originally had vehemently demanded immediate and drastic change had this to say:

>*"Paul, you are amazing. No one has ever come in from the outside, fitted in so quickly, and made such a positive contribution so soon.*
>
>*And it's clear to me how you did it.*
>
>*The others came in to SCORE.*
>
>*You came in to LEAD!"*

Secondly, here's the agenda you should always be pursuing if you want to rise to the top of any organization. It's one that most people will never even think about!

There's Power in Being 2nd Choice. Pursue the "If Not Me" Objective.

Stand by for the single most useful and profound bit of career-development advice I can possibly give you. It's not something you specifically *do* to get ahead.

Rather it's a way of living your corporate life among your peers that will speed and maximize your progress upward through the organization.

"Who do you think should be our next..."

In all matters, consider the effect your behavior is having on your peers. Throughout your career there will be many times when you will be a candidate for a promotion that should go to you or a peer. Prior to the actual awarding of that plum, there's a strong likelihood that the Board, the CEO, or your boss at whatever level will have informal discussions with all of the most promising candidates...you among them.

Each will put forth his or her reasons why he/she should be chosen. Your peers—if they are at all worthy—will surely have the self-confidence, as you will, to make a strong case for why ***they*** should be selected.

And after each has been given a full and fair hearing, chances are the decision-maker will then say something like this:

> ***"And if not you, who would be
> your second choice?"***

Here's where—let's hope—you come in.

Expect everyone to feel he or she should be the one best choice to get the promotion. "But," the decision-maker will ask, "who do you think would also be worthy of consideration?" I hope you've behaved day after day, year after year, within the organization so that your name will top the list of second choices. If so, you'll have an excellent chance of being chosen.

The decision-maker wants a top performer, of course. But he or she wants someone who will be favorably received by the organization. And that's the person who's identified by asking, "If not you, who?"

You can't be everyone's second choice if you have not done an outstanding job in handling your responsibilities. But you also cannot come-in-first-by-coming-in-second if you have engaged in petty political activity attempting to become #1 by trying to make others look inferior.

Here's where having been a team player and a fundamentally decent human being really pays off in business.

Example: A CEO I served many years as an executive recruiter had a team of six Presidents, each doing an excellent job of running his or her business unit, and all six units were very close to the same size. The CEO asked me to do an inside/outside search for a COO who would become his designated successor.

My job was to interview and assess all of the internal candidates, in addition to looking for outstanding outsiders with records at least equal to the remarkably good performances most of the insiders were turning in.

To my surprise, there was no internal candidate that more than one of the other six could abide as a potential boss. Indeed, several of the six asserted that they would leave rather than report to any of their peers.

Result: The CEO recommended, and the Board ratified, bringing in an outsider! It needn't have been so.

> **And now let's examine the most frequently useful problem-solving concepts you'll continually consider. These are the ones that come up most often in my practice.**

Look for Change!

What has changed? What else may soon change? If you're always on the lookout for change, you'll often find it.

Obviously you must know what everyone else in your field knows. If you don't, you're incompetent. If you do, you'll elude the firing squad. But you won't be special.

Only if you're aggressively looking for the earliest indications of change, do you stand a strong chance of being among the first to discover a potential problem or exploit an emerging opportunity. Only then will your business lead rather than follow the trends in your field.

Questions to Ask Yourself as You Look for Change

Continually scan the entire landscape of technology and business methods. Emphasize your own field, of course. But are there any developments in seemingly unrelated fields that might have application in yours?

Watch customer needs and attitudes. Are any new problems or desires beginning to surface?

Consider the needs, frustrations, and satisfactions of your own workforce. Can you provide advantages that others do not?

Be alert to how your superiors, peers, and subordinates are reacting to you at work. Might they understand you better or appreciate you more? Should you watch your back?

Be sensitive to the way family and friends are behaving toward you as well. Please don't become paranoid. But the line between paranoia and empathy is exceedingly fine. Relationships—both business and personal—can be nurtured far more easily than they can be repaired!

Are You Willing to Delegate?

You can never get everything done if you insist on doing it all yourself.

Worse, you'll never develop a successor who can take your place so that you can be promoted.

You simply must delegate enough major work to a subordinate so that his or her accomplishments will shine as proof that (1) you can pick, mentor, and lead good subordinates, and (2) you can be awarded a higher-level job without damage to what you're currently managing.

Are You Fearless of Good People?

Who should you delegate to? Obviously the best person you can find.

Face it. If your company, division, or department is to perform notably well, you've got to assemble the best possible team to run it. So what, if one or even all of your subordinates are equal or even superior to you?

If the business unit you are responsible for can turn in an outstanding performance and if the reason for that performance is that you have found truly excellent people, placed them in positions where their stellar talents will be best used, and empowered and encouraged them to do their best work, your superiors—and if not they, then outside recruiters—will be eager to apply your leadership to an even bigger business unit or perhaps the entire company.

No one was ever promoted because "he has nobody under him who is quite as good as he is."

Plenty of people have been promoted because "I don't know how she does it, but she surrounds herself with terrific people and gets absolutely the best possible performance out of them."

Hate Waste!

Reduce scrap, spoilage and shrinkage, and you'll widen margins and increase profit. You'll be a hero.

Provide attractive and comfortable working conditions for all of your employees at every level, and you'll increase loyalty and productivity, reduce turnover...and increase profit.

But indulge your personal taste for undue luxury

or allow your subordinates to indulge theirs, and you're headed for the wrong kind of attention.

Count on Murphy's Law. Just when you're in the corporate jet soaring toward a destination of dubious urgency is when the CEO will discover a totally unanticipated need to fly. And just when you've settled into your first-class seat on a commercial flight, you'll look up and make eye contact with your superior shuffling onward into a cheap seat. You can't afford such an accident. Why risk it?

Set An Example

Whether it's your subordinates or your children, you can expect them to be far more influenced by what they see you do than by what they hear you say.

Want to see a sense of commitment and urgency? Then demonstrate one.

If you want your subordinates to nurture and develop their people, take a direct, personal interest in the people who report to you.

Relax...Prove You Can Take a Vacation

Business today is more demanding and stressful than ever before. Therefore, it's important that you take time off to refresh your mind and body with nonbusiness pursuits. Use your allotted amount of vacation time. Plan ahead. Let superiors and subordinates know you'll be away and make specific arrangements as to who'll-be-doing-what during your absence.

Believe it or not, a well-planned vacation that occurs without difficulty is likely to be noted favorably. It demonstrates that you've got your responsibilities well staffed and organized. It may even imply that you're ready for promotion.

A series of intended vacations that are aborted because your responsibilities can't be covered in your absence proves just the opposite.

The corporation has no means of conferring sainthood. Leaders are promoted. Martyrs are oppressed even further.

Take a vacation!

See the Big Picture

So you're not yet the CEO. Nonetheless, if you want to get ahead, you'd better begin today to think as if you were. Indeed, always observe and think as if you were already managing the larger entity into which your unit fits.

If you were managing the larger unit, what approach to your unit would you take? Would you pour on the resources because it represents a superior growth opportunity? Or would you shortchange it in favor of another more promising unit? How would you view its requests for capital? Would you make strategic acquisitions? Would you invest in long-term R&D?

Perhaps you would divert investment *away* from your unit. Perhaps even starve its promotion. You might even increase its short-term profitability in order to dress it up for divestiture.

Nothing more clearly and indelibly marks an individual as bush league and unpromotable than if he or she demands resources and attention for a business unit merely because he or she is in charge of it. Don't make that mistake. Offer creative suggestions that can maximize shareholder value. Always think of the big picture and fit your area of responsibility into it.

Be a Switch-Hitter

Here's another way to view the big picture. Take advantage of every opportunity to work closely with your colleagues in other business units and functional departments. Volunteer to cooperate. Share information and resources. Be the person in your sector that others from other areas realize has taken the time to understand and appreciate what they do.

Perhaps a promotion opportunity will open up. Someone will be chosen to run both your area and another that you have taken the trouble to understand...a related unit where you've made yourself known and respected. Now *there's* a promotion that has your name on it!

Face it. Business runs in cycles. After a boom comes a recession, with its inevitable and painful downsizing. You may be one of the rare people the company can reassign—or even promote—as the pink slips fly.

Mind Business...and Only Business

Keep your mind, eyes, and hands strictly on business, and keep your mouth tightly shut on sensitive nonbusiness matters. A sexual harassment suit can do as much damage to an otherwise brilliant business career as getting caught misusing money or confidential information. Resist any temptation to aggressively share your religion or your politics with your business associates.

Your position in business gives you power. Don't use it for anything but business. You'll be sorry if you do!

Minding Your *Own* Business

Don't think for one moment that you can move yourself up in the organization by pulling others down. Sure, you see opportunities to criticize what your peer is doing with the unit he or she is responsible for. But keep quiet!

Bringing up the shortcomings of others merely encourages retribution. The person who previously had no reason to scrutinize and denigrate what you're doing now has a powerful motive to do so. And bystanders who might have trusted and respected you before will now have second thoughts.

When you take a gratuitous swipe at even one of your colleagues, your second choice "If-not-me" status goes right out the window!

Pave the Road to Outside Opportunity

Make yourself and your achievements "findable" by leading executive search firms. As you may know, I've written a comprehensive book on just that subject.

Believe it or not, you'll do far better work for your current employer knowing that you could, if necessary, go elsewhere. The self-confidence and serenity that come from knowing that every few weeks or months you'll hear about an attractive alternative to your current situation will encourage you to be frank and creative...not timid nor a sycophant.

Your superiors—or your Board, if you're CEO—will want to hear your frank assessments and your realistic plans. If you're confident that you can always get another job, you'll feel strong enough in yourself and in your overall career situation to deal in truth and realism, even when you might wonder how palatable they may be. Do that—albeit subtly and discreetly—and chances are that you'll stand out from your more timid and un-assertive peers, who merely echo the prevailing view and seldom present original and challenging thinking.

Make Your Boss Look Good

There's absolutely no advantage to be gained in trying to draw attention to your boss's shortcomings. After all, he or she has a boss...probably the person you are hoping to influence. Of course, you *might* hope that, once your boss's boss sees your boss's shortcomings, you may be promoted into your boss's job.

Don't count on it!

Perhaps you can succeed in undermining your

boss with his or her superior. Maybe you can even get your boss fired. But, suppose you do. Will you then be perceived as the kind of subordinate your former boss's boss wants reporting to him or her? Not likely!

If filled from within, expect your boss's spot to be filled by a less hazardous subordinate than you have proved to be...filled by someone who has minded his or her own business. And if you are the only logical inside candidate, don't feel too smug. An executive recruiter's phone is about to ring!

Absolutely No Surprises!

Don't ever go to a major management meeting with a presentation or an agenda that will come as a surprise to your boss or to any other involved party.

Here again is a way to distinguish yourself as *not* a team player...to mark yourself as someone to be watched out for.

Your tactic may succeed in embarrassing or maybe even mortally wounding some poor vulnerable

soul. But will it move you ahead? Usually not...
for all of the reasons we've just discussed.

Don't Hog Credit. Use It!

You're an executive. Your job is to get work ac-
complished by others...not by doing it yourself.

If your company, business unit, or group does
well, that overall achievement reflects favorably
on you.

If any of your people makes a noteworthy contribution to that success, his or her doing so is a credit
to your selection, training, and motivation. Generously give credit where credit is due.

Your able subordinate will become even more

enthusiastic and loyal, because he or she will surely have had at least a few superiors who behaved just the opposite way.

And the sheer self-confidence you demonstrate in handing off the accolades will enhance your image as a leader in the eyes of your superiors.

Your fairness will also be seen by other potential employees within the company. Nothing says "leader" more loudly than the clamor to enlist under his or her banner.

Justified credit awarded to your subordinates is one of your most valuable resources.

Don't waste it on yourself!

Do a Timetable. Back-Time Everything

You know when the end result is needed. And you know every component and preliminary step that will comprise the whole.

Take the project apart. Which aspects must precede which others? How long will each take? Which can be done simultaneously? Which must be sequential?

Wishing will *not* make it so. Only a detailed plan can do that.

Are you too advanced and important to do the

interval thinking yourself? Maybe so. Then put someone else to the task and take a look at their work. Or have someone you totally trust handle the oversight.

Sure, if you are building a skyscraper or a nuclear submarine, you will always have an exquisitely worked-out timetable. It's the seemingly simple objectives that don't get back-timed to perfection. And they need it too!

Juggling the TO DO List

There are some things you can really make a quick, positive, and major impact on. They are important—and therefore highly leveraged—and you can see exactly what needs to be done.

Act!

Juggle the "doable" things to the top of your list.

And keep juggling the list. Keep the rotating scanner of your mind continually glancing at the other matters that you realize need action or correction, but what to do about them is—as yet—

unclear or perhaps utterly perplexing. Or very possibly in need of corrective action that, although obvious, is too tough and unpopular—or too radical or politically incorrect—to pursue without laying more groundwork for it.

As you get into the habit of continually scanning the "to do" list of your work and your life, you will find that your list begins to juggle itself in a most useful and beneficial way.

Problems that were seemingly impossible to solve begin to show signs of weakness...vulnerability... chinks in their armor. You haven't yet figured out how to blast away the whole problem, but there is a piece of it you can chip off.

Do it!

The rest of the problem will drop to its—now— rightful place at the bottom of your list...or at least lower than before.

Do this and see what happens to your productivity...and peace of mind...and self image...and the way others regard you.

Sculpting David

Of course, juggle your TO DO list.

But that's not enough. You've got to cut it down.

You can't do everything. Don't even try. Figure out what's essential...and also what's so very desirable that it's nearly essential.

But what's merely optional shouldn't even *be* on the list. After all, "optional" means it's something you may or may not do, if and when you happen to have time and feel like it.

You need spontaneity and surprises in your life to make it interesting. If you bog yourself down with the psychological weight of a lengthy TO DO list containing unurgent things that you may never do, you'll continually feel frustrated...perhaps even guilty.

Lighten up! Clean out the clutter! Narrowly focus priority analysis and planning on a very tightly edited list of genuinely important matters.

There's a story about Michelangelo and his statue of David that illustrates the point perfectly. I can't imagine that it's true, but I'll share it with you anyway.

Supposedly a viewer of the great artist's masterpiece turned to him and said, "It's magnificent! How did you ever create it?"

To which Michelangelo is said to have replied, "Well, there was this perfect block of marble. I just removed everything that wasn't David."

That's the point. Try to remove—from your work and your life—everything that isn't David.

Include Murphy's Law in All Thinking

"If anything can go wrong, it will go wrong."

Professor Murphy was right. So get real. Anticipate the inevitable. Allow time for it, as you do your back-timing chart, which leads with certainty to the desired result at the right time.

If, by providing for possible slippage, you come to completion somewhat early, no one will fault you for exceeding the goal. Virtually anything that is ready early can either be used to advantage sooner than expected, or can be delayed, fine-tuned, and tested—often to great benefit—until the exact

TIME arrives.

One thing I can tell you with absolute certainty is that most executives do **not** consistently meet or beat target times. Those who do are prized and promoted when the others are not.

Let Your Mind Work Nights.
Do Your Creative Thinking in the Morning.

You probably have already figured this one out and are using it to great advantage. However, in case you have not, let me give you this tip.

Believe it or not, your mind works while you sleep. And what it seems to work on is an answer to your most perplexing problem of the day before. Perhaps, for example, the outline and the opening paragraph of that presentation which has had you utterly stumped for more than a week.

So let your first priority every morning be to bring

to a conscious level all the fine work your mind has piled up for you just below the surface. Because last night's work-done-while-you-slept is ephemeral, it quickly perishes...crushed and crowded out by whatever else you think about as your new day begins.

Every day your mind has worked overnight to deposit valuable new thinking into an "In" basket that will be empty within a few minutes or an hour.

Either you empty the basket by harvesting the overnight output of your subconscious. Or you address less important matters, and the basket empties itself, only to be quickly refilled with shallower thought on more immediate matters.

I state this suggestion to you, based on my own personal experience, and on scores of conversations on this very subject with executives and creative writers over many years.

I have no idea whether psychologists and other scientists have studied this matter or not...nor what, if any, conclusions they may have drawn. So many people have told me this process works in their life—as it does in mine—that I must share it with you, regardless of whether there's any truly scientific evidence to support it.

Choose Quality

Often the marginal added cost of a higher quality item or service delivers far more value than the threshold cost of a similar item of lower quality.

In the long run, the better item may even turn out to be cheaper. Its superiority may spark greater demand, which may lead to economies of scale.

There are many ways that a decision to go with quality may be rewarded in the future. And often those benefits are unforeseeable at the time the decision must be made.

Certainly there are *risks* when an opposite decision yields a third-decimal-place better gross margin.

Product recall, anyone?

Peter Drucker provided a valuable tool when he popularized Management by Objectives in 1954. Early enthusiasts pointed out that if, *for example*, an enterprise were to grow 15% a year, it would double every five years.

Wow! That paradigm had vast appeal. Suddenly, every management team was setting the same ambitious growth target, which—let the record show—the eminent professor had not personally espoused.

For a few years, merely by challenging themselves, managements were able to produce a level of performance they heretofore had not even thought of attempting.

But fairly soon the Druckeresque concept of doubling the size of a business in 5 years by producing 15% annual sales growth became unsustainable. Even with the help of inflation, which enthusiasts almost never adjusted out of their numbers, the steroidal top-line goal could not be met.

What then?

"Well," said many managers during the late-'50s,* '60s, and '70s, "if we can't keep the top line compounding at 15% a year, we can at least keep profit growth on the sacred continuum. All we have to do is find productivity improvements and lower-cost materials and components."

Again, a good strategy *in theory*. But hard to achieve...and capable of being carried too far. "We've been making it out of metal," said the over-the-top Drucker acolytes, "Now let's make it out of plastic. Also, where we had five inspections, now let's have two."

Meanwhile, the Japanese were studying not only Peter Drucker, but also W. Edwards Deming. We all know the result.

As kids, you and I read how, "For want of a nail, a kingdom was lost!"

The manager who chooses quality because he or she believes the customer deserves it and is bright enough to recognize it—or the lack of it—is going to be far more successful than the one who doesn't.

---

*Professor Drucker's 1954 book, *The Practice of Management*, is credited with popularizing the concept of Management by Objectives.

Plan Rewards

Pay fairly and even generously. Obviously, to attract the best calibre of employee, you'd better provide pay and working conditions that are among the finest available in your field at your location.

But hold something in reserve. Unless, of course, you're under a collective bargaining agreement. And maybe even then. Plan rewards for effective and loyal service that will be out of the ordinary and—if possible—unexpected and deeply appreciated.

Spend some time and thought on what can be

done to make working for your organization more interesting and rewarding than toiling for the competing employers all around you.

Is it stock options or grants? A bonus system that rewards (1) personal, (2) team, and/or (3) business-wide goals? A particularly appealing company car? Day care? Flexibility as to hours and workplace? An educational benefit for the employee or his/her children?

Or maybe even a degree of autonomy to do whatever the person thinks is appropriate to satisfy the customer without consulting a manual or appealing to higher authority?

There are many examples of unusual success in hiring and holding outstanding employees through the use of each of these devices. Surely you can think of a variation on one of these themes that fits your circumstances.

Whatever you do, try to include a reward that sets you apart from competitive employers. Capturing the attention of better people and keeping them longer can be a huge competitive advantage.

Welcome Diversity

Sure, diversity is fashionable.

And yes, discrimination is illegal.

But you want diversity in your work force for *other* reasons.

Your customers come in all colors, ages, genders, sexual tropisms, ethnic backgrounds, sizes and shapes. Your management team will have a hard time anticipating your customers' desires and respecting their sensitivities if you only hire and promote people like yourself.

The same diversity must extend down the ladder to the people who meet and serve your customers. How do you imagine they *feel,* if your organization seems eager to take their money but not to hire people from their group?

Don't expect wide-ranging creativity and customer rapport from a just-like-you management team and work force. It won't happen!

Be Honest

Why does this item appear so late on the list?

Why indeed even bring it up?

Isn't it obvious that, as they say, "Honesty is the best policy"?

Honesty had better be *more* than just a policy. It had better be your constant core value. If it's merely a policy, then that policy is subject to change whenever circumstances suggest a different and—for the time, at least—a more advantageous policy.

Forget about any spiritual dimension you may or may not believe in. You are constantly being observed and evaluated here and now. Anyone... your Board, your superiors, customers, vendors, family, friends...*anyone* who sees you take an ethical shortcut with a third party is *put on notice*. You may do the same with them.

Never put yourself in that position. Live your life and perform as a manager without even considering dishonesty—or a conveniently grey area just this side of it—as an option.

Sir Walter Scott said, "Oh, what a tangled web we weave, When first we practice to deceive!" He was right, of course.

Relax. There's far less stress and tension in honesty than in its opposite.

Respect Education. But Do Not Worship It!

I can't begin to tell you how many executives are toiling away seemingly endless hours in pursuit of an advanced degree, merely because they feel that the additional credential will open doors to them that would otherwise be shut.

For the young person just beginning to establish his or her career, this line of reasoning is valid. Indeed, *do* approach the world of work with the finest education you can afford.

But if you are already rather far along in your career—far enough to have learned *by doing* the line of work you pursue—give yourself credit for what you have already learned and achieved.

Recognize that most companies—and certainly the wisest and most practical—will hire and promote you for what you have proven you can accomplish, not for a degree that merely suggests but does ***not*** prove the potential you may have.

Not all superiors—nor all companies—will think this way. But the best ones will. And if you're in an environment where achievement doesn't count for much, you'd better go somewhere else.

We all know, but usually forget, that Bill Gates, Steve Jobs, and many others never completed an undergraduate degree...much less an advanced one.

Far too many people are slaving nights and weekends to achieve an advanced degree. They are stretching themselves almost to the breaking point writing a thesis, when spending the same amount of time writing a superior ***resume*** that would clearly show the outstanding work they're already doing for their current employer would pay far greater dividends sooner.

Yes, if you've gotten your career off to a slow and unpromising start, an advanced degree can be—as one wit once described a Harvard MBA—the River Jordan. It can wash all your sins away and give you a fresh start. If that's what you need, go for it.

But if you've been working awhile and have scored impressive accomplishments, make them known. That's easy these days, as I cover in a book I'll suggest later on.

Make sure you are working for an organization and a management team that recognizes and rewards a superior contribution. And then devote your nonpersonal time and effort wholeheartedly to doing an outstanding job for your current employer. Get recognized and promoted for the good work you're doing.

If you're not getting the recognition you deserve, MOVE! Document your results in a great resume and, as my grandmother used to say, "Take your pigs to a better market."

You cannot possibly turn in the outstanding performance needed to rise above your peers if you are merely coasting along at work, while devoting large amounts of time and effort to the pursuit of a degree that may be largely irrelevant after you achieve it.

Here's a test. Are you already making more money and handling more responsibility than is normally accorded to a person newly graduated with the advanced degree you covet? If so, the better course may be to forget the degree and get on with your career.

Respect Performance...Not Credentials

Here we flip to the opposite side of the coin we just examined.

Not only should you want to be evaluated on the basis of your performance rather than any extraneous credential, no matter how prestigious, but *you'd* better evaluate the people *you* choose and lead the same way.

Sure, if you don't have an M.B.A. or a Ph.D., it may nourish your ego to have lots of—or perhaps only—such prestigiously prepared people working for you. I've known plenty of managers who think that way.

The golden rule applies to employment and management, as well as it does to anything else.

If you want to be judged strictly on the merits of what you achieve, you'd better be prepared to evaluate your subordinates and your entire work force the same way.

Otherwise, a marketplace competitor or a management team colleague who *can* be objective will outperform you...and leave you smug, but eating his or her dust.

Value Technology

Is there an easier or better way?

Is there a technological development in your field—or in an entirely different field that might be adaptable to yours—that could increase efficiency, improve quality, lower costs, or speed results?

You won't be rewarded in the marketplace or in the eyes of your Board or your superiors for being behind the times. Whatever you're in charge of, make sure it's state-of-the-art.

The old saying used to be, "Be not the first by

whom the new are tried, nor yet the last to lay the old aside." As the syntax reveals, that is truly an *old* saying. It was wise indeed when Alexander Pope penned it in the 18th century. But that was then and now is now. Technology and business move far faster today.

There is still an advantage in avoiding a false start. But the penalty for being late in adopting a new technology is far greater today than Mr. Pope or anyone else could have imagined in the earliest days of the Age of Steam.

Don't Re-Invent the Wheel

Always ask, "Is there already a stock or an adaptable program, chip, or component that will serve your purposes fully or nearly as well as a custom-developed one?

Often you can be quicker to market and/or more cost-efficient by using something that already exists than by developing or specifying your very own whatever.

Also, why "go it alone" when a joint venture might be more efficient? Why not outsource whatever service or process a vendor can do better or more economically?

There will always be opportunities to take advantage of something that exists, rather than develop or build it from scratch.

Be on the lookout!

Think Ahead

Always be thinking about the *ideal* embodiment, even though you're up to your chin in getting out what's urgently needed and clearly feasible right now.

Today you're feverishly working on Version 2.3. What should be in 2.4, 2.5, and 2.6? And when should you be ready with 3.0, 4.0, and beyond?

The best way to evaluate what you're doing now is to keep one eye peering deep into the mists of the future. Day after day, we see new confirmation of the old saying, "What man can conceive, man can achieve." When you're not looking, you won't find.

Always Think From a Zero Base Line

Is *this* what we'd be doing if we were starting from scratch?

Perhaps not.

And if not, it's decision time.

Should you devote more resources to patching and improving the admittedly less-than-ideal product, system or strategy? Or should you modify substantially what you are doing? Should you begin anew, building on a better concept or strategy?

It isn't easy admitting that you, or your division, or the company you lead has made a mistake. But, after the flawed strategy or unseized opportunity becomes obvious, the sooner you do something about it the better.

Promoted To Take Over a Mistake?

Chances are that several times in your career, you will be promoted to clean up a mess in your own company. Or you'll be recruited from the outside to repair a bungle elsewhere.

Watch out!

Hopefully, your predecessor who was responsible for the blunder has been tossed out and is not around to become a potential enemy as you expose his/her folly. Great! You've got a free hand. You can be open and decisive!

But if the boss who's just promoted you or brought you in from the outside is substantially responsible for the mistake, be careful. Now you've got to get the necessary outcome—if you possibly can—without damaging him or her in the process.

Loyalty and decency have a big payoff in the corporate world. No, not always! Obviously not. But always, *under these specific circumstances.*

Senior executives above and around you—those who can do you the most good in the future—always have a keen eye open for loyalty. They won't speak of it to you or to anyone else. But when they're filling a lofty spot reporting to them, the fundamental nature you have demonstrated *will* be remembered. Even years later, it may give you an unmentionable but powerful advantage over the others you're competing with for a job everyone wants.

A display of smartass virtuosity is your first impulse when you get promoted.

Don't succumb to it!

Always Have Your Own Personal, Secret Plan B

As a leader, you must display confidence in—and enthusiasm for—the strategy or program you are leading. Otherwise, how can you expect your followers to follow?

But always have a "Plan B." Keep it in a secret, private part of your brain visited, perhaps, by trusted superiors you are comfortable sharing it with, but *never* by the troops you are now ordering to storm the hill.

Sometimes, if you have enough resources, you can openly pursue both plans at once; for example, you may put two R&D teams to work on different formulas...both promising.

But whenever the mission is absolutely critical and only Plan A can be supported, you'd better be ready to switch to B just as soon as it becomes absolutely clear that A is no longer a realistic bet.

Think MEASUREMENTS

Continually look for ways to quantify the performance of the business or sector you lead. Compare it to norms...industry, overall company, leading competitors, alternative applications of capital... whatever. You get the idea!

Make sure your comparisons are impressive. Then *volunteer* your "report card," even when it hasn't yet been demanded. There is no better protection against being underestimated, underappreciated, underpromoted, and undercompensated, than to let whoever controls your destiny know how very special you are.

And the best—indeed the only acceptable—way to "blow your own horn" is with numbers and other objective factual comparisons.

Never describe worthiness—your own or your business's—in mere words. Silence is preferable to adjectives. We can't trust your purely subjective evaluation, because you're biased!

Facts, on the other hand, (presumably) don't lie. Fortunately, however, they *are* susceptible to being very skillfully displayed.

Seem Smart At Math (1-Minute Course)

With no formal training, I began my career in consumer products marketing, and was soon supervising Harvard and Wharton MBAs, who consulted their slide rules during meetings. (Yes, that was 40 years ago!) Of course, I was intimidated.

I needn't have been. They dubbed me a numeric savant, because, without visible aid (pocket calculators hadn't been invented!), I often summed up discussions:

> *"In other words, about one in every 16 people has that problem."*

I barely escaped from lowest-level required college math. Fortunately, however, my fifth grade teacher insisted we learn the decimal equivalents of fractions.

Surely you already know them. But if not...

50% = half, 25% = 1/4, 12.5% = 1/8, 6.25% = 1/16 and 3.125% = 1/32.

Seem As Smart As You Really Are

Now we're into topics you may not need—or *realize* you need. Corporate mentors often ask me to cover these delicate matters with specific individuals.

Don't be underestimated because of conquerable hold-backs:

Foreign Accent: If you have one, you may not realize how impenetrable it can be to some people and how irksome, even if decipherable, to others. Fortunately, the problem is correctable by a good speech therapist. She or he won't wipe it out entirely (unless you're a passionate student) but can very soon reduce it from a communication barrier to a mark of worldly sophistication.

Hair Piece: Although women's go unnoticed, men's are a serious handicap to their wearers, who see them only frontally...and through a haze of glib advertising. They scream "insecurity," and that's not what a top executive wants to communicate.

Prepare for the Spot Light

Public Speaking: Forget about rising to corporate stardom if you're not comfortable making presentations and speaking off-the-cuff.

CEOs and other mentors often tell me the protegé they're referring is a "poor public speaker." If so, there's no quick fix. Serious work is needed. But there's always a pay-off in career progress and personal fulfillment.

I have two solutions. The costly—and less effective—is to put the executive under the wing of a no-longer-A-List actor who has a studio, video equipment, and a high pain threshold.

The other—far more effective and cheaper—is to send the executive to Toastmasters, the venerable nonprofit Alcoholics Anonymous-like organization that holds group sessions at which people from all walks of life practice giving speeches. The ambiance is congenial, hard-working, unthreatening, and nonjudgmental.

The results are often astonishing. A former boss of mine was not only a great business presenter, he was a TV-worthy stand-up comic. Always asked to MC corporate galas, he was hugely entertaining on every occasion. I asked how he developed his amazing skills and he openly admitted, "I owe it all to Toastmasters." While still a middle-manager he realized he was severely handicapped as a public speaker...a bore in stand-up presentations and a wimp in conference-table banter. "I knew I'd never get ahead if I didn't fix that," he said.

And fix it he did! He could have become a Leno or a Letterman. Instead, he settled for CEO of a Fortune 500 corporation.

Face it. You cannot be promoted to a major position—and certainly not to CEO—if your superiors today and your Board tomorrow cannot relax as you mount the stage or face a tough TV reporter.

Communicate Straightforwardly.
Let Mr. Lincoln Be Your Guide.

Would you like to have one of these labels tattooed on your forehead?

"I'm genetically programmed never to rise above middle-management."

"Don't waste your time talking with me. You'll get clearer information quicker from my boss."

"You probably think I'm uneducated, so I inflate my conversation with big words to suggest otherwise."

"I talk in generalizations, never specifics, because I've spent more time with academics than with business people."

"I come from a lower-class background and have never seen how very simply and clearly upper-class people communicate."

"I have a rotten self-image and feel that just being myself without affectation would reveal how insignificant I really am."

Of course you wouldn't want to label yourself like that. Nobody would.

Yet that's what a great many people do when they choose to communicate—orally or in writing—with long show-off words instead of short, clear ones. Or they habitually use broad generalizations instead of specifics. Or they ramble on instead of coming right to the point.

"U and non-U" words. In the 1950s there was a lot of discussion about the different terms for the same thing which are used by upper-class and non-upper-class individuals. The idea originated in the U.K., but it was studied and proved equally true in the U.S. People from families with wealth and education for generations tend to use simple, down-to-earth words. Poorer, less educated, upwardly striving individuals tend to use more complex, pretentious language.

Today, it's politically incorrect to comment on the phenomenon, but it still exists. If you think it may apply to you, get on the Internet and study some articles about it. You're not likely to become a CEO if you don't sound like one. And, surprising as it may seem, plainer—not fancier—speaking is what's needed.

Buzz words, psychobabble and jargon. Similarly, using plain English, rather than the vocabulary of your specialty is essential if you are to rise to the top. The language of CEOs is clear and generic. Learning to speak it early in your career will help get you promoted over others in your specialty who can communicate with their peers, but not with the generalists above them.

Habitual, grandiose generalization. Lethal to meaning, this disease is often contracted in college or grad school. Its victims convert meaningful specifics into pretentious vagueness. They say:

"A substantial and diversified portfolio of economy-priced consumer hospitality units in the Northeast."

...when they could as easily say:

"A $130 million group of eleven Holiday Inns and nine Super-8s in New Jersey."

If you have this tendency, ***get over it***. Until you do, prying facts from you is a frustrating ordeal.

Abraham Lincoln Got It Right

On November 19, 1863, part of the Gettysburg Civil War battlefield was dedicated as a cemetery for the fallen soldiers. Edward Everett, considered one of the greatest orators of that era, spoke for two hours.

President Lincoln, carefully chose and edited just 272 simple words and spoke for only two minutes.

Everett's monumental effort, full of pretentious words and flowery phrases was forgotten almost as soon as it was delivered. Lincoln's plain words are remembered. Indeed, they are considered one of—if not *the*—most eloquent statements in the English language.

So don't look down on simplicity. Appreciate it... and try to achieve it.

Avoid Badmouth Identity Transfer

Here's a phenomenon you may not have thought of. But it's real. And it's extremely important to your success in business.

Whenever you talk to someone about another person—and especially if that person is in a role your listener can relate to—your listener hears your comments *as if they were about him or her*.

If you speak derisively about your current subordinates to a candidate you're trying to hire, don't be surprised if he or she doesn't sign on.

If you're interviewing for a position and speak negatively about a current or former boss, don't be surprised if you're not hired.

People are alert—consciously *and* subconsciously—for clues as to how you'll think about and treat them if they become involved with you.

The best evidence, of course, is what you're saying about others. Be careful. You're saying "him" and "her." Meanwhile, your listener—considering your words and *personally trying them on for size*—is hearing "I" and "me."

Yes, such a transference might be totally unfair. The person you describe may have dire failings that are well known to everyone who has ever had first-hand experience with him or her. But your listener has had *no* experience, one way or the other.

So watch what you say. It absolutely must sound objective and reasonable. If it can also (when true) sound respectful, appreciative, loyal, and supportive, so much the better.

Harness the Power of Doing What You Said

Years ago, I did a search for a President of the CBS Television Network. There were no logical candidates at the other networks, so my likeliest prospects were the presidents of the major movie and TV production companies.

Grant Tinker, then CEO of MTM Productions, immediately became the person I most wanted to attract. His reputation was unique in Hollywood. "Everyone takes their concepts to him first," said my informants. "*Afterward*, they submit them to the other studios."

Wow! Someone who'd get his pick of all the new program proposals before competitors saw them! He'd be ideal in a business where success depends on getting the best shows. "That's astonishing," I said. "Why is it so?"

"Because he listens to your pitch and then he says, 'We'll give you our decision in two weeks.' *And he does!* A 'Yes,' of course is fabulous. But so is a 'No' in just two weeks. Other studios will also promise you an answer in two weeks. But they *never* do as they say. Probably, six months later you still won't have your answer...and meanwhile, you're tied up. You can't take your property any-where else."

This principle has many applications. Become known for reliably delivering what you promise. Chances are, like Tinker, you'll stand out from the crowd. Customers and vendors will favor you. Superiors will depend on you...*and promote you*.

If you're wondering how the story ended, CBS decided to promote from within and soon became #1 in the nation again. But a couple years later, Grant Tinker became President of NBC, which then zoomed to #1.

Who Are Your Potential Successors?

You've got a lot better chance of being promoted if whoever controls your destiny is sure there's someone who can step in and do your job successfully.

An empty box on the organization chart is a problem. If upping you creates a *new* problem—then you may be stuck right where you are...capable of a higher job, but never getting it.

Here's a tip I give all my recruiting clients. Fortunately for my profession, very few CEOs and other senior executives follow this very logical plan:

Periodically (at performance review?) ask your key subordinates to name, in priority order, the top three prospects they're grooming to take over their job and the pros and cons of each one's readiness. Ask, too, for the names of at least four executives at industry competitors who are worthy of consideration. What are their reputed strengths and weaknesses?

Any good manager (1) grooms subordinates and (2) keeps an eye on the industry's notable talent. Formalizing that process will pay big dividends.

Showcase Your Stars!

As we've just seen it's very much to your advantage if whoever is in a position to sponsor or approve a promotion for you knows that there is someone who can step in and take over your current responsibilities.

Therefore, when it's time to make presentations to the people you report to—whether divisional management or the Board of Directors—you'll have your key lieutenants mount the platform and point to the charts. You won't relegate them to the extra chairs at the back of the room.

Less formal opportunities to show off your key

people abound. Let them become known by name if not by face. Reward the producer of a cogent "white paper" on an important subject by sending it upward with merely a brief cover memo from you, or perhaps just a handwritten comment on the front page. Resist the temptation to remove the writer's fingerprints and create a glory trail that only leads back to you.

Having been generous, prove that you were. Send the writer a copy of your cover memo or a photocopy of the hand-annotated cover sheet. Your subordinate will be delighted that you are winning him or her important recognition. Working for you is not only a pleasure and a learning experience, it's also a road to advancement.

There will be a good buzz about you among the entire echelon of managers beneath you, not just those who report to you. (Bosses *are* talked about.) Others will be eager to work for you whenever an opportunity arises. And your ability to "cherry-pick" your team will almost assure that its performance will recommend you for a promotion.

Of course, it takes guts as well as generosity to behave this way. A sleazy subordinate might try to take advantage of the recognition you've facilitated and attempt to undermine your position with whoever's above you. If you haven't seen *All*

About Eve, the 1950 Mankiewicz-directed Bette Davis classic, rent it.

Of course, there's some hazard. But, if you're going to pick and support the wrong people and then put up with disloyal behavior, nothing I write here can shield you from trouble.

A Really Outrageous Idea

For many years there was a senior executive at General Electric Company who absolutely amazed me with his willingness to recommend his own best people when I called him as an executive recruiter asking for suggestions.

Invariably he'd say, "Well, the #1 best person I have for that job would by X; the second-best would be Y; and third would be Z." Then he would proceed to elaborate on the advantages and disadvantages of each. Finally, he would offer to tell the ones I seemed most interested in that they should expect a call from me.

Was this fellow nuts?

No. He was a brilliant and highly successful manager. Over the years, I probably presented at least a dozen of his people to my clients. They went to their interviews. They got offers. But not a single one of them ever left GE. In the end, they couldn't leave a boss—and because of him a company— that so obviously respected them and cared about their professional development.

Times have changed. So have loyalties. Today, there's little loyalty to a corporation, because corporations seldom show much loyalty to their people. But ***there still is loyalty to an inspiring leader***...to a fine executive. Indeed, personal loyalties are the glue that holds employment relationships together these days.

If you're a leadership virtuoso, you may want to carry the loyalty / leadership principle to the extreme. You may want to recommend your best people when a very few of the finest recruiters you personally respect and want to cultivate call you for suggestions.

Make Yourself "Findable"

Speaking of executive recruiters, let's elaborate on something I mentioned earlier. You really should make it a point to become personally known to at least one top recruiter in the largest firms and also to some of the very prominent individual recruiters in the prestigious "boutique" firms.

You couldn't possibly have read this far and not have realized that I have a bias that says, "You're better off, if you stay with your current company and rise to the top there." Much of this book has been about the best ways to accomplish that objective.

Recognize, however, that even the best managed

career in an absolutely outstanding company may someday blow up.

There's always the possibility of an acquisition or a merger. Then, the combined entity is not going to need *two* CFOs or, indeed, two of almost any title you may aspire to...all the way up to CEO.

Downsizing, too, is a spectre that emerges with every ebb of the economic cycle. Someday it might bring you a pink slip. Or—let's be optomistic—a lucrative buy-out offer.

Clearly there will be times when both you and the company will benefit if you have a wealth of personal contacts in the upper realm of the recruiting industry...if you are already known and "in-demand."

Rites of Passage and RiteSite.com

Here disclosure is required. I am the author of *RITES OF PASSAGE at $100,000 to $1 Million+,* and also the proprietor of its related Web site, RiteSite.com, which publicizes searches by outstanding search firms serving the high end of the market and helps senior executives make sure they're not overlooked when such searches occur.

I will make a few dollars if you take advantage of these resources. But I can't merely for that reason fail to tell you that, if you want to cultivate relationships with the top recruiters, *RITES OF PASSAGE*—at 300,000 copies and counting—is the #1 bestselling book on the subject with roughly 20 times the sales of its nearest competitor. Obviously it's helping people, and I hope you will take advantage of it.

Get Promoted Where You Are

Here's a fact that may surprise you. Your current company actually ***wants to promote you***.

No, not if your performance is less than outstanding. And not if your leadership skills, behavioral traits, and reputation in the organization are less than excellent.

But if you are capable of taking on more responsibility and handling it outstandingly, your company would prefer to keep your talents and get even more benefit from them. It would rather not send them off to strengthen a competitor. That is, of course, if it realizes how valuable and versatile you are and is continually thinking of higher-level assignments to develop you further and put you to better use.

But stop!

We're talking about a *CORPORATION* as if it were a *person* and therefore capable of recognizing its self-interest in dealing with you.

It's not, of course. It's a mass of people and capital doing business, making a profit, and paying compensation, benefits, dividends, interest and taxes. It may—let's hope—be employing skilled organizational development people in the HR Department whose jobs are to help the amorphous corporate organism think like a rational person about its management-level employees and the contributions, aspirations, and satisfactions of each.

"God Helps Those Who Help Themselves."

But even in a corporation with ideal organizational development and management succession programs, you should be doing some looking out for yourself.

Recruiters aren't the only path to a new and better job. *Networking* is the #1 job-changing method.

And there's no reason to apply it only outside your company and only when you're unemployed.

Make a continuing effort to know and cooperate with other key people throughout your corporation. Being widely known and respected piles up valuable "If-not-me" points (see p. 22). It also may help in time of need. At just the right moment, you may be recruited for a great job in another part of the company by someone who realizes you must hate your obnoxious new boss or who sees you endangered by a rumored merger or downsizing.

Recruiters are a wonderful career resource which all senior executives should cultivate. But almost every recruiter-generated opportunity requires relocation...and a host of other bothers and uncertainties as well.

Staying where you are has obvious advantages. But you've got to do some independent self-assigned work to make sure you share in them.

Consider Your Wild Card

What is the thing that absorbs your time and energy that is utterly personal and perhaps secret to you? It could be as private as an illicit relationship or as public as an obsessive need to witness every home game of the Chicago Bulls. Either way, it's probably something that you and I would never discuss if I were your executive coach.

Is it worth the investment in time and emotion that you give to it?

Probably you can't give it up immediately. But did I say, "Give it up?"

No. My advice—and this you easily *can* follow—is merely to *consider* it. Consider it as you enjoy it. Put it into clear perspective in comparison to all the other parts of your life.

Gradually, you *may* become a bit less interested in it...a bit less committed to it.

Feeling guilty and saying I'll never do *that* again is no way to ease your commitment to your Wild Card. You simply can't stop it "cold turkey." It means too much to you.

But drop your feelings of guilt entirely. Let this activity and your thoughts about it into your regular routine life. Think about your Wild Card in the very same way you think about everything else you do.

Watch.

As you develop objectivity about your Wild Card and matter-of-factly consider its actual importance to you in comparison to everything else in your life, you will probably see your compulsive need for this activity receding in importance.

Will you give it up? Should you? Will it stay precious to you, but just consume less of your time and emotional energy?

Who knows?

Nothing Is As It Should Be

No other observation in this book is as perpetually relevant as this simple realization:

Nothing is as it should be!

Think about it. It's absolutely true. Nothing is ever what it optimally could be. Your job, your subordinates, your relationships, your marriage, your children, your parents, your health, your looks, your home, your financial situation...the weather.

OK. You've read three paragraphs By now you

are already seeing the profound ***truth***—and also the *falsity*—in that too-sweeping statement.

Sometimes something—the weather, for example—*is* perfect...just as it should be. And sometimes virtually anything else in your situation can be about as satisfying as it possibly could be.

But that's not always.

Indeed, it's not usually.

Accept that fact. Understand that most of the time almost everything could be better. That's the nature of the world. And of our lives, both business and personal.

And there are only two things you can do about it.

Get busy and take action on all the not-as-good-as-they-could-be things that you have the power to influence.

And relax. Chill. Get realistic. Accept what you cannot change. Try to do so with humility and a sense of your place as one among many lives on the planet. And also—if you can rise to the challenge—do so with a *sense of style*...knowing that you can be special in some way, despite the irksome banality or fearsome chaos that surrounds you.

A truly brilliant observer has pointed out that there are two types of people in the world. Some think that the world is a 5-star hotel and are continually complaining about the room service. The others think that the world is a prison and are continually marveling at how really pleasant it is.

Who are you? Who would you rather be? Who do you think derives more satisfaction and enjoyment from existence?

If you can put your circumstances into perspective. If your reaction, rather than frustration and perhaps even a sense of hurt...or injustice...or in today's fashion, victimization, can be to accept and analyze the facts of the situation, then you'll probably come up with a plan. You'll see things you can do to remedy or at least alleviate the situation.

And if the situation is one that you cannot or for valid reasons you should not—at least at this moment—attempt to change, you can allow it to recede into the background.

Achieving profound realism is not an easy talent to cultivate. But it's a talent every one of us has.

Work on it!

Epilogue:
at Journey's End

We're finished.

I hope you've enjoyed our excursion together and, along the way, have seen some of the landscape—although familiar—from new perspectives.

We've covered a lot of ground, including many of the strategies we'd implement together if we had the luxury of working one-on-one.

Everything we discussed was pared down to its briefest essence. Therefore, much of it went right into memory, as further calibration points on the chart and compass that help guide your successful senior management career.

A business psychologist friend of mine who's probably the #1 authority in that field confirms that brevity helps ideas stick in the mind. However, he also suggests you reread this book occasionally. John Drake* says, "An individual is a different person at different times, and their changed circumstances will change what they absorb from what they read."

"After the first reading," he says, "put *JOURNEY* on your night table. It's a book that will yield new insights after each reading."

He has a point. Hopefully, we'll meet again on these pages.

Meanwhile, thank you for our time together...and very best wishes for outstanding success and profound satisfaction.

Sincerely,

John Lucht

---

*John Drake is the founder of Drake Beam Morin and, after retiring from that firm, also of Drake Inglesi Milardi. Both are outstanding Human Resources consulting organizations.

*Please see page 103
to order this book.*

About the Author

John Lucht is one of America's foremost executive recruiters. Since 1971 he has been bringing senior executives into major corporations in the U.S. and overseas...as head of The John Lucht Consultancy Inc. in New York City since 1977, and for six prior years at Heidrick and Struggles, New York, where he was an officer. Earlier he had a successful career of 10 years in marketing and general management with Bristol-Myers, Tetley Tea, and J. Walter Thompson Company.

Lucht is the author of RITES OF PASSAGE AT $100,000 TO $1 MILLION+...THE INSIDER'S GUIDE TO ABSOLUTELY EVERYTHING ABOUT EXECUTIVE JOB-CHANGING, since 1988 the world's #1 bestselling book on executive job-changing and career management, and of the EXECUTIVE JOB-CHANGING WORKBOOK, also the leader in its category. These books are supplemented by RiteSite.com, a no-advertising, entirely service-oriented Internet site.

Lucht's consulting practice is no longer limited to executive search. Since 1990 he has been doing personal and highly confidential outplacement and executive coaching of very senior executives. He also lectures and gives seminars on management and career issues and is an expert legal witness on career, employment and compensation matters.

A New York City resident since 1960, Lucht grew up in Wisconsin and received his B.S. and Law degrees from the University of Wisconsin and its Law School, where he also taught Legal Writing.

Turn Page to Order This Book

Share *INSIGHTS FOR THE JOURNEY,* which has been called...

"...the ultimate executive development and counseling resource"

Martin Gutfreund, Senior Vice President -
Human Resources and Administration
Uniroyal Technology Corporation

If you are with a corporation or a nonprofit and wish to *share* *INSIGHTS FOR THE JOURNEY* within your organization, you may order copies in cartons of 24 delivered by FedEx. No charge for shipping and handling, and we absorb and pay all sales taxes, where applicable.

To order by *phone* call:

1 (800) JANUARY

Or order *online*:

InsightsfortheJourney.com

This book is available at all fine bookstores. Please support your favorite local or online retailer when purchasing less than 24 copies.

ISBN 0-942785-31-2.   HARDCOVER, $19.95

NOTE: This book is not—and never will be—available in any paperback format.

*Please see page 103
to order this book.*